Far Away

John Crawford

D1528451

As Always

For My Beloved Wife Bette Baj Crawford

&

To Those Who Go To The Dark

&

Come Back With The Light

&

Live To Write About It

Other Writings of John Crawford

"We Had Today"

"A Widower's First Year"

"Alone Together"

"The Widower"

*

"A Child's Tear"

Under the pseudonym Leo Tracy

All available through Amazon

4   *Far Away*   *John Crawford*

Pages in Back Pocket   *Page 5*

Prologue   *Page 23*

I'm Anxious Mr. Bergman   *Page 23*

The News Anchor   *Page 60*

She Came Back To Me   *Page 76*

Alone In Car   *Page 98*

Dear Bette   *Page 111*

Love Letter   *Page 127*

Love Letter   *Page 155*

Bette's Old Guy   *Page 171*

Pages In Back Pocket

Saint Peter

The man looked in my direction and waved back with a smile. A minute later he left his bar stool and walked towards me.

The man: What's up?

Me: I know you are him.

I looked at the confused expression on his face. I started to feel anxious.

The man: What are you talking about?

Me: Oh, I'm sorry. I thought you would know me. I should introduce myself. My name is Jesus.

The man: And mine is Napoléon. What's going on here?

Me: Your time has come, once again, to be a 'fisher of men and this time women'.

He looked around the bar to see any big ass grins or hear a guffaw from any of his buddies and none came.

The man: Who put you up to this?

Me: I don't know what you're talking about.

My sincerity gave him pause.

The man: My name is Paul.

Me: As I said my name is Jesus and may I call you Peter.

I didn't flinch. He took a moment.

Peter: Sure, that would be fine. What is this about?

Me: I work in a bookstore but my main job is building a religion.

Peter: How is that going?

Me: The book selling not bad and the religion is a work in progress but I am getting there with a little help from my friends.

Peter: Good to hear. I'm a professor of Russian Literature at Yale.

Me: I graduated Yale three years ago with a degree in social work. I don't remember seeing you on campus.

He seemed impressed with my alumni status.

Peter: I started a year ago.

Me: My favorite novel is Fyodor

Dostoevsky's "The Brothers Karamazov".

Peter: That's interesting. His novel is the reason I'm a professor of Russian Literature.

That blew my mind; our being on the same page and considering the novel is roughly 900 pages that is a lot of 'same pages' to be on.

Me: My favorite character is the young monk named Aloysha and as we both know he is devoted to spreading the message of Jesus.

The features on Peter softened and I didn't want to see it but sure enough, the look of pity. I did not need that look.

Peter: And mine is Ivan.

Me: I am not surprised considering he is the intellectual mouthpiece for Dostoyevsky. But you do believe in me don't you?

Peter: We can talk about that. I hope I'm not too forward in asking you about being under Doctor's care and maybe on medication; now don't take offense.

Me: No I understand. To doubt is quite natural. I must ask you to take a leap of faith. If you do so it will help us communicate.

Peter: I must tell you that sadly I have to turn your offer down to be a 'fisher of men and women'. It is too big a job for me.

Me: You are too modest. May I offer a verbal prospectus?

Peter: If you keep it brief because I have a class to prepare for.

I know his staying was an act of charity but his loss would have hurt and I didn't want that.

Me: I want to make it easier for everybody this time. I want no beatings, no torture, and no crucifixions. I said it was time for the worlds' of God and Caesar to merge for the sake of all. Ensuring quality of life will be the prime objective.I went on for a couple more minutes about bringing the 'twelve' together again and how the use of the Internet would expedite the process of spreading the 'Word'. I told him I believe there is more suffering now than ever and We would be more generous in making miracles. The faces of hope are everywhere.

Peter: I wish you all the luck in the world with that.

I was feeling nervous about failing to convincing my Peter to try again. Curiosity and a kind heart kept him at my table but I could see he was ready to leave me. As he stood to walk away I grabbed his arm; too hard I'm afraid. He pulled away and backhanded me with open hand and his college ring drew blood from my temple. Immediately, I saw regret.

Rose the kind woman behind the bar saw what happened.

Rose: Paul come on he's just a kid.

Peter: Rose I know. It's ok. It's just a scratch, kid.

Me: I'm ok. It's very difficult for me to let you go.

Peter: I understand and let us talk a little more about the religion your building. I will be right back; need a refill?

Me: I'm good thanks.

Peter went to the bar and talked with Rose.

Something inside me thought he was stalling for time but that was okay; he was here.

He was curious about where I lived and I told him in the hearts of my people. He asked for more information about the religion. I told him about the importance of music and it being God's language. He leaned forward and asked me to name my favorite composers.

The voice in my head said,

'go ahead let Peter have his fun but beware'

Peter: A top twenty would be cool.

The 'voice' was compelled to comment after mention of each composer's name.

Mahler – 'He is taking you for a fool.'

Beethoven – 'He is just killing time for the police to arrive.'

Mozart – 'You chose wrong.'

Bach – 'That would explain the betrayal.'

Schumann – 'He doesn't appreciate the urgency of your words.'

Mendelssohn – 'He is not going to follow you.'

Brahms – 'He has set in motion your capture by the guards.'

Wagner – 'The true Saint Peter is still to be found.'

Strauss, Richard – 'You have failed in the day's mission.'

Puccini – 'There will be other days.'

Elgar – 'He may come back to you.'

Sibelius – 'You can reconsider at that time.'

Nielsen – 'You will have to deal with Lucifer soon.'

Tchaikovsky – 'Lucifer harbors so much envy for you.'

Shostakovitch – 'Your Father may have asked too much of you.'

Prokofiev – 'The Cross may be too heavy a

burden.'

Ives – 'The children, I know, the poor children.'

Copland – 'Yes, the search for Saint Peter will continue.'

Barber – 'And His will be done'

Bernstein – 'On earth as it is in Heaven.'

My back was to the bar entrance and I did not see or hear the Police until they were right behind me. I heard the cop say the cuffs were for my safety and my insistence on leaving quietly without handcuffs seemed to matter little. I am strong and as they grabbed my arms to put behind my back I pulled away and knocked over the table where Peter and I were sitting. I now had everyone's attention.

Out of the corner of my eye I saw the strong hand of Paul my   Peter intercept the nightstick swing of the advancing cop.

Peter: No need for that.

The cop was taken aback and angry.

Peter's next motion was to put me in a harmless bear hug and urge me to be calm, go with them and all will be fine. His assurance both physical and emotional brought all resistance to a halt.

I heard him say to one of the cops.

Peter: Your chief is a friend of mine and this man's name is Jesus and I'm sure he will be safe while he is in your custody.

With my hands cuffed behind me I looked at the Yale Professor of Russian Literature and saw my Peter a decent man of integrity brush away a tear while I thanked him.

*

Jesus Is President

I fantasize about Jesus being President of the United States. He wins by a small margin.

In a matter of days, weeks and a few months 'The Infrastructure for Quality of Life' will soon be completed.

The results thus far are amazing:

Drugs and alcohol are much less a priority in people's lives.

The number of criminal acts perpetuated on people and property have never been low.

Extremist talk radio hosts have all been let go because the number of listeners is way down.

Sales of all manner of anti-anxiety and anti-depressant drugs have plummeted.

Fascist statements, jingoist statements, xenophobic statements, chauvinistic statements and homophobic statements no longer resonate with the populace.

Forums regarding civilization-humanity-evolution-true progress of the heart-true progress of the spirit are popping up throughout the nation from small towns to large cities. A real sense of pride of who we are as a species has never been felt like this on a national level.

All corporate mission statements are labor and environment friendly.

In the discussions that take place after

church services people are saying they feel at

peace whenever they are out in Nature as if the

planet is in a state of gratitude.

   Relationships and friendships have taken

priority over self-centered, greedy pursuits.

   Mansions are considered lonely houses.

Modest homes are engaged in block parties where

dwellers celebrate community.

   Television commercial advertisement is dirt

cheap now that reading, reading clubs and playing

of musical instruments is at an all-time high.

   There have been sightings of magnificent

luminous white auras over the animal preserves

throughout the continents.

   Judging from the inner peace most people

acknowledge and the numerous acts of kindness

being witnessed I'd say we have been touched by

the Holy Spirit and are in a State of Grace.

*

State Secrets

Bette

You know the truth is not all it's cracked up to be. I'll give you an example.

A few days ago I saw a guy on the ward who held on to a rolled up newspaper like it was a matter of life or death. We found out later that was the case, in his mind that is. Other patients kept pestering him to give up the paper and he refused. The patients complained and a couple psychiatric aides walked towards him. He bolted down the hallway to the bathrooms. He must be thinking they are going to take the paper from him. A minute later I hear him yell "The fate of the world is in my hands; I can't let you have the codes."

I hear a scuffle and then silence. The next thing

is the bed on wheels being rolled into the day room

and he is in four point, wrists and ankles, restraints.

I saw him crying as he lay there tied up

watching the newspaper being separated by

sections and passed around.

I found out later his delusion was being a CIA

operative whose mission was to safeguard the

nuclear codes encrypted in the lines of the

newspaper and having failed in safeguarding the

newspaper his country was now at risk.

I am so fucking angry.

You should have seen him not only in tears but

a look of fear for what will become of his country

because of his inability to protect the codes.

Why not let him be in his delusion. He is doing

no harm. The psych aides can go get another

goddamn newspaper or two for the other patients.

(Bette paces)

John

That was me.

                    Bette

I know.

                    John

You talked about me like I wasn't here. That's upsetting.

                    Bette

I am so sorry. I wasn't sure you would remember. Sometimes the medications block memory as you know. What do you have by the way.

                    John

What do you mean?

                    Bette

What is your diagnosis?

                    John

They don't know.

                    *

Prologue

I received an email from a magazine saying they would like to publish my short story "I'm Anxious Mr. Bergman".

Bette was in the hospital. She was nearing the end of her corporeal life.

I didn't want to be away from her so I asked my sister Pat if she would contact the editor and have the magazine sent with my story, special delivery, as soon as it was available.

Bette didn't see the magazine.

*

I'm Anxious Mr. Bergman

My Psychiatrist's name is Max Bergman, a hell of a nice guy, and his name may be the reason I chose him from the list provided by the insurance company. He stands six feet with a stern look and gray hair in a crew cut.

There was a Swedish film maker named Ingmar

Bergman who I admire and on occasion in fits of inebriation I blame him, the church and others for my obsessive thoughts regarding: God, Life, Love, Death, Meaning, Destiny, Despair, Joy, Sadness, Cruelty; it is a 'blame' of high regard.

I see a psychiatrist because of acute anxiety. It has been a longtime companion.

At the end of our first session Mr. Bergman asked me to prepare for the next one by recollecting, in as much detail as possible, the first time I felt profoundly anxious about something.

I agreed.

I had hope in the telling that some healing will be provided.

I am 23 years old as of this writing.

When I was seventeen years old, during one of my visits to Uncle Bill in Greenwich Village, Manhattan, NYC I went to see Ingmar Bergman's film, "Cries and Whispers". It was during the middle of the film when I felt fear.

I don't want to think it had to do with Bergman's movie. I like the films of Bergman.

I'd like to think the anxiety came on all of a sudden and for no particular reason.

*

It was early Saturday morning and the smell of Spring coming through Uncle Bill's fifth floor window; fighting the city smells was inspiring.

I couldn't wait to get outside and enjoy Washington Square Park.

Over a breakfast of scrambled eggs, toast and orange juice Uncle Bill brought to my attention the Bergman mini festival being held at "Cinema Village" . He knew I liked Bergman and suggested we see a film together in the evening.

He would be back from his audition for Biff in "Death of a Salesman" and we could do dinner and the movie.

I looked at the list of films and said I want to see "Cries and Whispers".

Uncle Bill looked at the schedule and said it was only showing Saturday afternoon.

He apologized for not being able to back out of the audition. I said that was okay and I understand.

I told him I didn't mind seeing it alone. He heard the film was pretty deep and to make sure I had my thinking cap on.

"Hey John why don't I take you to an Off-Broadway show tonight. I have a friend in the production."

"Sounds great."

*

"Wild Strawberries" was my first Bergman film.

I had a difficult time explaining to Eddie, my best friend, the identification I felt with a character who is a dying 78 year old Professor/Physician.

Eddie could get serious at times and being no

dummy said it was probably less the old man who is charmingly irascible but more the theme of the film' Know thyself'.

Bergman took Socrates' dictum to heart; "The unexamined life is not worth living".

I agreed with Eddie considering I was always questioning things from an early age. I needed to know the world and my place in it.

I told him I feel sad and discouraged when I think of a person having difficulty finding someone to talk to about serious matters like metaphysics, theology, philosophy etc.

I made him laugh when I said...

"A person broaches those subjects and there are no takers but let another person throw out an invite to catch a "Marx Brothers" film, and it is seized upon like a bear to salmon.

Mind you, this is not to say the serious person doesn't enjoy comedy and suffice to say the why's, what's, where's and how's of existence are usually

pretty good fodder for any stand-up."

"Here! Here!" Eddie replied.

*

Part of the thrill of watching a Bergman film is

the feeling of having stepped into one of "Dali's"

surreal paintings, where you find a boulder to sit

and you contemplate the symbols.

In Bergman's films along with the terrific

visuals you listen to a soliloquy or dialog between

characters which is usually about God, Love, or

Death and you also listen to the silence.

His facial close-ups are riveting and

intimidating.

*

I will have you know that day in Greenwich

Village at age seventeen I was a virgin and

extremely interested in the opposite sex. I could

have been down the street watching a comedy

with lots of 'tits and ass' but I chose to be here at
"Cinema Village" watching "Cries And Whispers".

I think about the question I had then and still
think about it; why the intense interest in
understanding my relationship with God and its
meaning.

I do suspect it has a lot to do with the Death of
Christ, His Resurrection, the Communion of His
Body and Blood, and the Cross/Glory of Witness
that was imparted to me at an early age.

As you can imagine that imparting (or maybe
better to say 'indoctrination') profoundly informed
my young Christian life.

Heck, what with daily Catechism, Sunday Mass
and being a devout Catholic altar boy how could I
not be held captive by my faith.

But

I do worry about doubt and how much of a
sinner it makes me.

I worry about doubt when I read or hear about the suffering of children and then I pray to a Loving God.

Sometimes I am overwhelmed with mystery and fear.

*

The theater is half full and I'm happy with my seat in the center of the middle row.

I find the film emotionally engrossing, intellectually stimulating and mystifying.

My feelings are influenced by my empathy for the character facing death.

I search for meaning.

Thoughts of death have a corner room in my mind and the door is always open.

Bergman is so good at elucidating finite death you may get desperate and look for an exit.

But

You stay loyal to Bergman and stay seated

Unless

The heart palpitations, sweaty palms and shortness of breath compel you to leave before Bergman's world ends.

I was confused, upset and angry as to what was going on with my body.

I wondered if my mind becoming fearful and anxious

Was

Taking it out on my body.

I had to leave.

In the lobby I held tight my sweaty ticket and told the usherette I felt a little dizzy.

Her name was Bette and her commiseration made her more attractive as she approached and guided me to her chair behind the concession stand.

"I feel dizzy."

"Oh, please come here and sit down; my name

is Bette."

"Thank you Bette. My name is John. Sorry to be a fuss. I don't know what's come over me."

"Your crying John. You okay?"

John in a whisper

"I'm not crying Bette. Beads of sweat got in my eyes. Please don't fuss."

"No fuss. Let me get you a glass of water."

"Thanks."

"You do look a little pale."

"I'll be fine. I just needed to get out of the theater for a minute."

"You don't like the film?"

"I love the film."

"Oh good. So do I."

"That's nice."

"I'm feeling better. I need just another minute."

"Sure, take your time."

I thanked her and sat with my head down

hoping my brain would get the hint that passing out was not an option.

A few times I raised my head to see her look of consternation and smiled faintly.

(Good choice of word don't you think?)

I'm sitting there in love with the movie yet fearful of hearing statements from characters that could shake my faith a little.

Any clue as to what was happening to me lay dormant in some corner cobweb of brain synapses that retreated from introspection.

The worry of a heart condition did exist but I dismissed it due to my youth, no history of heart problems and (son of a gun) I was starting to feel better.

I'm watching the popcorn maker. The kernels are popping and the smell of fresh popcorn with butter at the ready for pouring did not help any but there was nothing I could do about that.

So

I had a choice: walk out of the theater, onto the street and head back to Uncle Bill confused and worried about what just happened or go back to the movie confused and worried but determined to see the end of the film.

I thanked Bette for her solicitude.

"I'm going back now."

"Good. You haven't missed too much of the film and anyway I'm sure you will see it again."

"I'm sure. Thank you. You been very kind."

"That is nice of you to say. I always am kind to strangers."

"Lucky for me. I'll go now."

*

I, being a considerate fellow, got back to my seat with as little disturbance as possible.

I certainly didn't need additional anxiety on the off chance I caused a member of the audience to miss 'something'.

It was good to be back with Mr. Bergman and his sharing thoughts with me on selfishness and what lengths two sisters will attempt to avoid confronting mortality in the mansion of their dying sister.

The 'saving grace' is loyal Anna, the maid, who comforts the dying sister to the end.

I tell you Dr. Bergman; a despicable bunch are we if not for the Anna's of this world.

*

After watching the film for awhile my first emotion was anger with myself.

I couldn't believe my palms; the sweating. Soon to follow were heart palpitations and shortness of breath. Whispers of 'flight' echoed in my ears.

But

Staying in my seat became a thing of pride. To ride out the dismal situation became a priority.

A silent cry for help to Jesus brought tears. "Cries and Whispers" wasn't getting the attention it deserved and I felt awful.

But

I hoped to prevail and was doing just that when all of a sudden nausea came on the scene.

I know most people don't like to vomit but I really, really don't like to vomit.

The chance of being sick in the theater and creating such a mess, not to mention the utter disturbance and embarrassment, I had no choice but to surrender.

By the way

Over the years the "Be sick and get it over with, you will feel better" exhortation from Mom never did break my resolve to avoid the toilet hug. After taking the pink anti-nausea liquid I would pace and distract myself in any way possible waiting for the magic potion to do its trick.

Pink is one of my favorite colors because of what it helps me avoid. I have a few light pink shirts.

I told Eddie who also became my financial counselor that when I have disposable income I want shares of 'Pepto-Bismol' stock.

I'm sorry, I digress.

SO

I knew I wasn't coming back; the possibility of vomiting saw to that.

I made a quick exit to the lobby, nodded to the usherette Bette and left the theater.

In addition to being confused over what just happened to me while watching "Cries and Whispers" I also felt guilty for not saying a nice goodbye to Bette.

She was cute. She was kind. I think she liked me.

I let go the opportunity to make a friend.

I like sharing my thoughts.

I don't know why.

I worry they won't like me.

I think I make too much of rejection.

Maybe we will meet again.

I head for Washington Square Park looking for a diversion. I like pigeons and was glad to see them enjoy the food left by people. I sat on a bench and watched them pick and pop food into their mouths. I like the way they walk.

'People watching' can also be a diversion but today it held little interest.

I perceived a 'normalcy' among the people. I was envious. They could sit through a Bergman film.

But

Would they want to? I don't know.

But

I couldn't sit through the Bergman film today

and I was bothered by that in a big way.

What kind of crap is that.

So

I sit there watching the pigeons and avoid looking at people and fuck the psychology of what happened in the theater; what about the damn physiology.

The mind trips over itself and the body falls down.

Shit. When I felt nervous in the past there were no physical manifestations.

Now

I got the sweaty palms, the heart palpitations, the shortness of breath, and the nausea. What else could happen?

Ticks, seizures, blindness, coma, shouting obscenities, memory loss...

A strange kind of clinical fascination was building.

Today there is something new to worry about.

I wonder when the anxiety and need for 'flight' will happen again.

I thought of this.

I'm in a boxing ring. I am on the ropes. This is getting real physical. No more 'mind games'. 'It' is going straight for the body. It won't let up. There is no hitting back while I block the blows holding my arms up to my face. There is no more 'fight' in me. 'Flight' is my only option.

*

I left the park,the pigeons, the faceless people and walked up Fifth Avenue. I stopped at the end of every block to look up toward the Empire State Building.

I thought of this.

Now that would be some 'flight'. And then

I thought of this.

Not until all the fight is beaten out of me.

*

*I went into a diner and ordered coffee and an
English muffin.*

*With a little something in my stomach I started
to ruminate more on the psychology and less the
physiology of what happened in the theater.*

*Something in the movie pulled a trigger that
shot a hole in my mind. Cold air was let in on the
warm subject of my death.*

From an early age

*I knew that in order to cope with death I had to
make it my friend. I did with the help of Jesus.*

*In the film a cold, lonely, eternal death hung
over the film like a delicate, porous, transparent
swath of cloth providing no warmth or comfort.*

I was left transfixed, scared and empty.

I was bothered

*by the film raising questions about the afterlife.
Did my anxiety and eventual 'flight' provide a*

retreat from Bergman's questioning.

Did I fear succumbing to doubt in an afterlife?

Did I fear questioning my faith?

*

Ingmar Bergman took the dictum of Socrates to heart

(Know Thyself)

and on a profound level Mr. Bergman summoned me to share in the conversation of life's meaning and purpose and of course death has to be part of that conversation.

His genius and talent asked me, encouraged me to contemplate life's themes of destiny, suffering, evil and beauty.

I met some demons in the film I know I wasn't ready to meet.

I must remember.

The work of an Artist is to present Beauty as a Calling; A Calling one to Home. There when we

close life's door for the last time the good bye will
be easier in having shared our home

*

God bless Mr. Bergman's compassion and grace
as a dramatist.

His words and vision provide us with the
instruments to dissect death and give us a better
understanding and appreciation of life.

The beauty of a Bergman film is that after the
movie is over and having hitched a ride on his
metaphysical wings you realize you have secured a
loftier place and despite all the pain and suffering
you are better for it.

*

My Uncle told me in the later part of Mr.
Bergman's life he no longer considered himself an
atheist.

I find comfort in that.

*

It is awful to contemplate the horror of dying alone.

It is even more despairing and devastating to imagine death as the last scene in the last act of the great play of one's life never to be produced again.

I can't allow myself to believe that.

There is no death only transition.

*

"Hi John"

"Oh, hi Bette the usherette?"

"Yes."

"You aren't stalking me are you?"

"I am John."

"You know there are laws..."

"I am aware but don't care. I wanted to see you again."

"You look beautiful, Bette"

"Thank you, John."

"What can I order for you?"

"Coffee and an English muffin."

"That is what I ordered."

"I know."

"You know?"

"I was watching you; that is what stalkers do."

"Of course. How silly of me."

"Don't say that."

"Say what?"

"Silly."

"Silly?"

"Silly."

"Why."

"It sounds 'silly' coming out of your mouth."

"Isn't it supposed to?"

"That's why you should not say it."

"You know what, Bette; I agree. From here on out the word silly will be banned from my vocabulary."

"Good John."

"Oh here is your English muffin and coffee."

I told the waitress to put it on my check.

"Yes. Thank you John"

"Your welcome Bette."

"Why'd you not say a proper goodbye?"

"I was angry, confused and upset."

"No reason to take it out on me."

"Sorry. You are right."

"After all I comforted you when not well."

"You did."

"I gave you my chair."

"You did."

"I gave you a glass of water while you were sitting in my chair."

"You did."

"And then you leave in a huff without a proper goodbye."

"I know. I am sorry."

"It was as if we had an argument. You do not know me. Did that make it easier to be rude?"

"Bette?"

"Yes John."

"Are you crazy?"

"A little."

"I'm sorry."

"It's not your fault. And you would be too if you had to listen to Mr. Bergman several hours in a given day."

"I don't know about that."

"Oh come on John who are you kidding. The man gave you a full blown panic attack."

"I suppose."

"You suppose nothing. You are not ready for Bergman. You are the guest he did not invite but you went anyway."

"I know. You are right."

"I know I am and I can tell you what went

wrong."

"Really?"

"Don't say that."

"What."

"Really."

"Really?"

"Really."

"Oh jeez. Are you going to continue striking words from my vocabulary?"

"If I must. Yes."

"You know, if I didn't like you I'd walk away."

"I know. Do you want to know what went wrong?"

"I do, yes."

"Okay I will tell you. As a young boy you were innocent and vulnerable with regard to religion. The instruction in matters of faith and morals kept you up at night. You grew up with Jesus dying on the Cross. Is that anyway for a young person to

live?"

"Thank you Bette for the insight. I'm not sure I agree but thank you."

"Don't thank me; thank yourself because you are the poster child for 'Indoctrination at an early age'."

"Ha Ha. I gotta go soon."

"I scare you John?"

"No Bette of course not."

"Good. That is the last thing I want."

"My Uncle Bill is expecting me and I don't want him to worry."

"Aren't your Uncle and I the same age; around 24?"

"Yes. Lucky guess."

"Not really."

"Hey..."

" And yes I can use 'really'."

"What are you saying?"

"I am your Uncle's girlfriend. I am in an Off Broadway show and he will be introducing us tonight."

"What?"

"He called me at the theater and asked to keep an eye on you."

"Did he say why?"

"He was worried about your response to the film."

"That's ridiculous. Why would he worry?"

"He told me you are a sensitive young man."

John looked at Bette and mouthed the words 'what the fuck'.

"I'm sorry we upset you."

"You followed me to the movie house?"

"I was already there. My Father manages the theater and I work there."

"Then you left there to follow me?"

"I did. My Father covered for me."

John looked at Bette and again mouthed the words 'what the fuck'.

"I'm sorry we upset you. And then you being panicked at the movie and the way you left; I had to make sure you were okay. I hope you understand."

"I do. Why didn't you tell me right away?"

"I was putting it off. I apologize."

"Accepted."

"And if you want John we never met until tonight."

"Tonight? Uncle Bill is taking me to a show tonight."

"Yes I know and I'm in the show; an Off Broadway production of "A Streetcar Named Desire". I play Blanche DuBois. He wanted to surprise you. He said you like Tennessee Williams."

"I do, very much."

"So okay then 'we never met'?"

"I'd prefer that, thanks."

"Sure. I better go. And we'll keep the cries, whispers and secret to ourselves."

"Bette, there is no secret in "Cries and Whispers."

"Silly boy. I know that."

*

I left the diner and headed for Uncle Bill's apartment.

I told him what happened at the theater.

He gave it a name; 'anxiety or panic attack' take your pick.

He understood when I talked about its raw power and the compelling need to leave.

He said one can be at a loss and not fathom why the body would succumb; betray the mind like that.

I agreed with him.

*

Bette was terrific in the show. Afterwards we went for pizza and had a fun time. We walked Bette home then went to Uncle's place.

*

"Bette is beautiful, Uncle Bill."

"She is."

"Does she love you?"

"Yes."

"And do you love her?"

"I do. A little forward of you, nephew."

"Yes. I feel entitled."

"I see."

"I talked with Bette at "Cinema Village"."

"I know John. She told me when you were in the bathroom at the restaurant. She felt she had to. Don't be mad at her."

"How can you be mad at Bette; such charm and knowing innocence."

"Tell me about it... Are you upset with me?"

""Do you mean the mothering hen thing?"

"Yes."

It was hard not returning Uncle Bill's smile; I succeeded.

"I am but I'm sure to get over it."

"Just looking out for you kid."

*

After getting home to Connecticut from my visit with Uncle Bill I researched 'anxiety attack' on the Internet.

I was not alone.

In the spirit of Sherlock Holmes , when it came to the attack, I brought 'deductive reasoning' to bear.

As soon as I felt the beginnings of one I retraced mental steps to the light and dark corners of my mind hoping to find a clue and maybe stop or lessen the attack.

There were a few times I was successful in

finding clues as to its origin and then keeping the anxiety attack at bay.

I believe the success had to do with the meager forces behind the attack. The anxiety proved weak.

The will to fight overcame the need for flight.

But

When the 'anxiety attack' forces were abundant, no matter where I was and provided no clues as to origin I hung up my Sherlock Holmes hat, gave up the fight and engaged in the 'flight' response.

*

Dr. Bergman thanked me for my candid courage in telling him about that day at Cinema Village attempting to watch "Cries and Whispers".

Before the end of the session I said a few more things. I worried that it may have been too much 'crazy' talk.

I said:

When I think, write and talk about my mental illness; it is all I can do to keep my head from exploding.

When I get loopy I feel the weight of what I'm saying should drop my jaw to my chest.

The desolate visions should cause interminable eye twitches.

The heated inner dialog should melt at least part of my face.

The scream of my impassioned words should be heard for miles and not on deaf ears.

I want my understanding to shed light on a dark, bleak, staid landscape for those who come after me.

I want to think of death without anxiety.

I want to live with the solace of knowing there will always be a tomorrow.

*

Dr. Bergman nodded politely and then...

he said:

Go 'Van Gogh' yourself John.

No more esoteric movies

No more existential readings.

No more isolationist ruminations.

Paint!

Find a meadow.

Lay on the grass.

Look up and see the tree branches giving life to the supple leaves

Look beyond the branches and leaves to the cloudy blue sky.

Lay your mind on one of those clouds.

Find your soul in the blades of grass, the leaves and branches.

Let the canvas reflect all your soul finds holy.

I thanked him and congratulated him on the nice wrap up to our session.

*

Latter...at the age of 25.

I wrote a brief letter to the good Doctor Bergman.

Dear Doc,

I have finally taken your advice and I am in the Virgin Islands.

In regard to painting I have no talent whatsoever but I still paint.

The canvas and palette of colors provide the opportunity to see and not question.

Sometimes that is healthier.

The Islands are beautiful and I am not alone. Bette is with me.

Bette and Uncle broke up.

Bette and I are now girlfriend/boyfriend.

Her insight and knowledge of Bergman's films is astounding and we brought twelve Bergman DVD's with us.

The hotel room has a good size screen.

The Bergman 'close-ups' look great and are no longer intimidating.

After each film we have a long, wonderful and invigorating conversation.

I am in love.

Sincerely,

John

News Anchor

Jack is nineteen years old with brown hair, blue eyes , six foot, looks like Randolph Scott and attending community college. He wants to anchor local news with an ambition to becoming a national network anchor.

Eliza is nineteen years old with blond hair green eyes, 5 foot, looks like Barbara Stanwyck and attending a four year college in the neighboring state. She is majoring in Criminal Justice. Thoughts of being a FBI agent interest her.

Eliza is in love with Jack.

Jack is in love with Eliza.

"She asked Jack why the interest in TV Journalism."

"Jack said, my parents are news junkies and watching news, especially local, is something I have been doing for awhile in the early evening.

I like that the good anchors display a genuine

gravitas when reporting serious news and that demeanor can help one connect to the community.

I want to be the compassionate link between the News and the Viewer."

Eliza said she believed he would do well in the job.

She asked if Jack could make a tape; reporting on their love affair. Jack was astonished and overjoyed.

"You love me?"

"I do Jack."

"And I love you."

He asked Eliza why the interest in the FBI.

"I have always been a reader of crime and mystery books and fortunately I identify with the good guys."

*

Jack and Eliza have been together a couple years. Recently she asked for a little 'space'. He was worried.

"Don't worry love. We are okay. I need to focus on my studies."

"Is everything alright between us Eliza?"

"Yes Jack. All is fine."

*

While Jack was walking home from class he witnessed a car accident. One of the cars came out of a side street and went through a stop sign.

He immediately dialed 911.

There were others in the area and they surrounded the two vehicles looking for an entry point that wasn't mangled.

As they approached there was an explosion and the car was in flames.

Jake and the others had no choice but to back away.

Before fire completely engulfed the cars Jack saw blood on the windows and could only hope sudden death spared them from being burned alive.

After answering police questions he walked to a bench behind the school library and sat for awhile.

He let go the tears he'd been holding since the accident.

He couldn't help but remember his Nana, his Grandmother.

A couple years ago he lost her in a car accident.

In the first twenty four hours of her hospital admission there was talk she might recover but a brain aneurysm put an end to that conversation.

Jack was devastated having lost the person who loved him as much as his parents and who laughed at all his jokes.

At age five Jack had a good head of hair which his Mother loved combing every day.

Having come home from the Barber with Nana

and entering the kitchen where his Mother was
Jack put his hand to the top of his head...

"Nice crew cut, Mom."

"Mom smiled then cried."

I am told it took a few weeks or maybe longer,
when the hair started growing back, before Mother
forgave Nana.

*

Mom said Nana's loss was like the cutting of
the other umbilical cord; the one tying her to the
universe.

Jack's Mom never got tired of telling him how
lucky he was to have a warm, compassionate,
intelligent Grandmother.

The hospital that Nana was rushed to is where
he met the candy striper, Eliza.

When Eliza first entered Nana's room there
was a conversation going on between Jack and his
Mom. Jack appreciably noticed how Eliza stood

near the door to give then privacy.

Nana's condition was serious and Jack could see the sad and solicitous look in Eliza's eyes. He could feel her empathy and wanted to know her.

"Hi this is my Mother Dee and my name is Jack and you know my Grandmother."

" Yes and I see she is resting. I'll come back latter...Oh my name is Eliza and glad to meet you."

"And you also, Eliza. You go to Wilson High?"

"I do. I'm a senior."

"Me too. I thought I've seen you."

"And I you."

Jack and Eliza have been a couple ever since.

They went to the Prom.

They go to movies, concerts, theater and ball games.

They have many long, deep conversations.

And

After getting to know each other very well they

made love.

*

"Hey Jack."

"Hey Eliza."

"I just read Jonathan Kozol's "Amazing Grace: The Lives of Children and the Conscience of a Nation".

"What you think?"

"Wow. I loved it. I'm going to minor in Sociology."

"Yeah."

"Yeah. The kids Jack. We must take care of the children. If we don't lift the children out of abuse and poverty; Christ stays on the Cross."

"I never thought of it that way, Eliza. It's like He is not truly Resurrected until we all live up to His Gospel."

"It's kind of how I been thinking about it lately, Jack."

"You take your faith pretty seriously."

"I do."

Late in her Freshman year Eliza told Jack she would go into Social Work if the FBI didn't work out.

*

Jack let his mind come to the present.

He prayed for the occupants of the car.

He was pretty shaken up and so glad Eliza agreed to meet him.

Jack hoped a month would be enough time for 'space'.

Eliza and Jack talked last night...

"How are you, Eliza?"

"Good Jack, and you?"

"Miss you a lot."

"And I you."

"Truly?"

"Yes. Time away from you Jack was quite

instructive."

"Oh. How so?"

"I learned that being away from the one you love sucks."

"Good lesson. Not talking to you Eliza has been horrible."

"Tell me about it; so many times I almost hit the speed dial."

"Me too. By the way I did put together a video reporting on our love affair. A couple friends helped me and I think it came out well."

"I can't wait to see it."

"When do you think?"

" I have no classes tomorrow."

"Tomorrow it is. The bench behind the library."

"The bench behind the library. 2 okay?"

"Perfect Eliza. My only class that day is at 11. I'll go home after class and put together a couple sandwiches. Hummus on rye okay?"

"Perfect and I'll bring chips and soda."

"A date, then."

"A date. See you then. Love you."

"And I love you, Eliza."

*

The video; "Eliza and Jack, the Love Affair" was made a couple weeks ago. Jack enlisted the help of a fellow Journalism student.

"And here we stand in front of the home of Eliza...

"Oh Hello. There are the parents of Eliza."

"Hi Jack. How are you?"

"I am fine Mother of Eliza. Would you mind being on camera and saying a few things about your daughter."

"We'd be delighted. Now where do we start. A terrible infant; colicky and you know how that goes. We gave her the nickname, 'enfant terrible'; such an unruly child. Don't even get us going on *her preadolescence years; she couldn't wait to be a teenager and as she said 'I'll really drive you crazy'."*

"Thank you parents of Eliza for the clear picture you presented...There you have it.

And here we stand in front of the high school Eliza attended...

And there are three of Eliza's girlfriends...

And what kind of girl was Eliza?...

"A mean girl."

"An inconsiderate girl."

"A spiteful girl."

"Thank you girls for your honesty; you can go now...There you have it.

"Oh there is Mr. Rooney, Eliza's English teacher...Excuse me Mr Rooney may I have a moment of your time to ask what kind of student Eliza was...

"I'd be happy to tell you. Eliza hardly paid

attention in class, chose CliffsNotes over reading the book, and homework assignments were incomplete. To be honest; a poor student without an ounce of ambition."

"Well Mr Rooney thank you for your candid assessment...You can go now...There you have it.

Later that night...

...Regarding "Eliza and Jack, the Love Affair" there is 'Breaking News'. I am reporting from my bedroom. It is unorthodox but-hey.

Now Joe, keep the camera on me not the pictures of Eliza-okay thank you-sorry folks for the tech difficulty so as I was saying "Breaking News'.

It is confirmed that Jack and Eliza talked earlier today and gladly Eliza has found her 'space'. She and Jack will meet tomorrow and close the 'space' between them. This is Eliza's doing and Jack couldn't be happier.

It has brought me great pleasure in reporting

this story and I'm sure the viewers along with myself wish Eliza and Jack the best of times. Good night and pleasant dreams...

Oh a minute please-Joe come over here please-yes the camera is to be on-all set?-good...

I have this note from Jack passed on to me earlier today by my co-anchor and I forgot it was in my pocket-apologies to the viewer...

Jack wants Eliza to know he is keeping a Journal and in that Journal are his thoughts on Eliza's beauty, intellect, charm, empathy, compassion and the love he feels for her.

He writes his love for Eliza grows stronger every day. He thinks of her as the ocean and his love for her and life is buoyed by her waters.

His love for her is horizon-less.

Thank you Jack and goodnight Eliza"

*

Jack hoped Eliza would like the tape. He truly

wanted her in his life.

But

Jack would ask nothing of Eliza she wasn't willing to give.

He thought back on the night they first made love. They stayed at a motel.

He thought about how tentative their touch was at the start and its evolving into holding tight; never wanting to let go.

The next day...

...His cell phone rang.

"Hi son. Where are you?"

"At the school. Eliza's coming down for a visit. I'm waiting for her. She should have been here an hour ago. Why?

"Jack Eliza has been in a car accident. Her car was being worked on so she got a rental and one of the cops said from eye witness accounts it seems the brakes failed. We are at the hospital."

*

Jack was in the same motel room where they spent the night together.

He believed he could smell her perfume.

He closed his eyes and saw her smile with such joy while wrapping her arms around his neck and pulling him down to her chest.

He saw thin rivulets of shower water on the soft white skin of her back.

He watched as she devoured the large breakfast.

She said, "No cigarette for me after love making; give me a hearty breakfast."

Later that night...

...He turned on the nightly eleven o'clock news.

"Sadly we lost one of our own today in a car accident on Weston Street by the college. Her name is..."

Due to the bourbon Jack could barely get his

eyes to focus on the TV.

But

He did hear genuineness, gravitas and empathy
in the New Anchor's voice

He hoped the earnest reporting brought some
comfort to those watching who knew Eliza...

And

To those who did not know her but felt a
connection through the news anchor.

*

Jack let out a scream meant for God's ears only.

He mourned for Eliza.

He mourned for his lost soul.

He couldn't feel less anchored to the
community.

She Came Back To Me

My nights are shorter at age 70. I go to bed early. My mornings are longer. I get up early.

I miss the nightly prime time dramas. My cable company has a feature called 'on demand'. I can watch shows at any time. I take advantage of that. All that being said the business of watching television alone is not appealing.

I have to say there is no appeal in doing much of anything alone.

I look forward to my dreams where I'm not alone.

I get old and my circle of friends diminish.

All my dead family and friends come to me in my dreams.

My subconscious is like a repertory theater for my beloved departed cast. They come of their own volition and take me on bizarre, mysterious journeys.

Once in a while I believe the person in the dream is sending me a message.

One dream where Mother and I are sitting at the kitchen table of my boyhood home I believe is a message dream.

She is young and I am old. She keeps saying how old I look.

"I am old Mom."

"Look at how young I am."

"I never wanted you to get old, Mom"

We talk about Dad and his working three jobs to keep our heads above water. She stops talking about Dad and suddenly...

"I love you son."

"I love you too Mom."

"Go get that colonoscopy for crying out loud."

"Yes Mom."

The next day I scheduled a screening and sure enough the exam showed precancerous polyps.

I went to church and lit a votive candle.

I prayed she would continue to watch over me.

*

I dream of people who I thought were alive.

I worry they may be dead if they are in my dream.

The other night I had a dream of Liz.

She was a co-worker I fell in love with a while ago.

She was attractive at 5', 105 lbs. with short blond hair and terrific posture.

It saddens me to think she may be dead.

*

We worked 3rd shift at a psychiatric hospital.

The hospital had immaculate grounds.

Liz said it was a fine place to be crazy.

I smiled.

After shift we spent many a morning walking the hospital campus.

My initial thought upon first seeing her....

"What the ... I am out of her league."

I try not to put much emphasis on 'looks' but our society sees it another way.

The first conversation Liz and I had dispelled that notion.

There was time to talk during the shift and we did.

She loved Country music and turned me on to it.

I loved Broadway Musicals and turned her on to it.

She was down to earth and self-deprecating about her looks.

She found me cute, interesting and a good listener.

I found out later how many signals of her wanting intimacy with me I missed.

"With my feeling unattractive it must be easy

to understand how I missed the cues." I said.

"Yes and no. Some might say you'd be more apt to pick up on the cues." She said.

She commented on my blushing and I blushed more.

"I am happy with all the conversations we are having and getting to know you Liz."

"And I you, John. Quite honestly your not coming on to me was quite the turn on."

"Who knew?"

"Obviously not you. It took a year for you to bed me."

"Mea culpa, my Lady."

"And now we're in love."

"Yes we are Liz. And the confidence I brought to our conversations I now bring to our love making. I thank you for that."

"No thanks necessary, sweetheart. I am a patient woman and you were certainly worth the

wait."

I was Joe DiMaggio to her Marilyn Monroe and I have never gotten over her.

"There is a God."

*

We were together for three years.

Liz and I enjoyed weekend getaways and more often than not we drove to Route 2 in Northwest Massachusetts; also known as the Mohawk Trail between the towns of North Adams and Greenfield.

Near the end of the third year Liz was diagnosed with precancerous cells on her cervix and needed a hysterectomy.

She broke off the relationship.

"John how can you ask me to stay with you when I know you want children."

"I love you Liz. I don't want us to part. We can adopt."

"I can't."

"What do you mean you can't."

"I can't be with you knowing I can not give you a child."

"If you leave me you leave knowing I didn't want you to go."

"I accept that John."

*

In the dream I had last night I find myself in the motel on Rt.2 we frequented the most. I walk into the room we stayed in and there she is smiling and saying she is happy I am here. She stands there in a white robe looking as beautiful as ever.

"How old are you love?"

"Twenty seven John."

"How old am I?"

"Twenty seven and you look great for your age."

"Thanks Liz and you also. We are the age when

we said goodbye. We are young again."

"Yes we are."

"You look real comfortable in that robe Liz. Do you have one for me?"

"Of course hon; in the bathroom. Can I get you a glass of wine?"

"Yes, please."

"You could have stayed away, you know that John."

"Why would I do that Liz."

"Anger."

"After all these years?

"Anger is a strong emotion and can have an impressive life span."

"I never stopped loving you, Liz. Did you marry?"

"No, John"

"And you?"

"No Liz. We should have stayed together."

"We didn't know then what we know now."

"No we didn't. I think of you every day."

"John, please."

"What. I can't say that?"

"I just asked you here to say goodbye."

"We already did that Liz. What's going on?"

"I'm sorry. It was wrong of me to enter your world after all these years."

"What do you mean? This is my dream. You're here because of me."

I pulled her towards me and wrapped my arms around her.

We made love.

*

The notebook was on the nightstand.

Upon waking I wrote down as much as I could remember. I was anxious I would forget something. I feverishly wrote down any tidbit.

I dozed off at times hoping I'd be back in the

motel room.

I stayed in bed till noon.

A couple hours later I decided to travel to the motel.

While I was driving a song Liz and I loved came on the radio. The song brought me back to her.

I pulled over and waves of memory swept over me like an emotional tsunami. I swallowed hard and tasted tears. The steering wheel remained intact under my tightening grip.

I forgot how much I missed her.

With the song over I pulled into a 'package' store and bought some bourbon and beer.

*

The motel hasn't changed much.

"Yes sir. That room is available. Your lucky day."

"Why is that?"

"A lady reserved that room for last night and tonight but left a little while ago; she wasn't feeling

well."

"Was her name Liz?"

"Well sir I shouldn't..."

"Please..."

"...Yes."

"I see...Well thank you."

*

I lay on the bed and looked up at the ceiling.

I worried about Liz.

I felt she would be back and I had to be here.

I hoped with the song fresh in my mind and the familiarity of the place; remembering Liz would come easy.

I got a glass of beer and a shot of bourbon.

There was an outdoor table and chairs outside in front of the motel room window. I sat there.

With little in my stomach it wasn't long before the 'alcohol high' set in.

I meandered along the memory lane of our

three years together. I was determined to remember every devoted look, caressing motion, devouring kiss and loving embrace.

Time passed.

I was getting hungry.

Liz loved Chinese food and cashew chicken in particular. I ordered two chicken cashew plates for delivery.

The sky was full of cumulus clouds which lent a kind of majesty to the day. The memory of our love awakened in me a youthful feeling; one where hope and possibilities prevail.

I thought I heard a noise coming from the room and I turned to look.

An old lady was sitting at the small table by the wall with a landscape picture above.

She is writing, head bent with pen in hand.

After a moment I turned away and sat very still not wanting to disturb the moment.

I started to feel anxious. I am not that drunk I thought.

I heard the door open.

"You lonely John?"

I didn't turn around. I heard Liz's voice.

"Of course not. You're only in the next room."

"I am, aren't I."

"Yes and it is all that matters.

We are old Liz."

"Yes we are John."

"Come on in. Lay down. Rid yourself of that 'little drunk' you got going on inside your head."

"Thanks Liz. It's a good idea. Don't go away."

"I won't John."

"Oh Liz?"

"What John."

" Do you remember when you would come out of your apartment wearing those tight denim shorts, riding a little too high, and I'd say 'there

asking attention of only me' and you say 'who else my love'."

"I do John."

There now go lie down.

"Do you remember when we would go to breakfast after work and then to the park we loved."

"I remember all our outings there."

"How about the time I was 'high' on philosophical writings and wouldn't stop talking."

"I remember and when I started to unbutton my blouse and told you I would continue only if you stopped talking; you kept on talking."

"What the hell was wrong with me."

"I thought the same thing.

And

the next night at work you brought in Nietzsche's "Also sprach Zarathustra" and asked if we could read it together."

"Yes."

"I didn't like the 'God is dead' part John."

"I know but I was so happy with the interest you showed in the rest of it, Remember?"

"I do John."

"Liz?"

"Yes, John."

"Before I drop off will you sit here by my side?"

"Of course."

"You let your hair grow."

"I did."

John gently caressed Liz's hair.

"I remember when you had short blond hair crowning your soft cherub like face."

"Hey! Is cherub code for fat?"

"Hell no. Next time I'll say angelic."

"That's better, I think."

"You know Liz some memories come easily to mind and others come out of no where; without

the asking."

"I know and I'm so glad we have them John."

"Yes. I wish we had more."

"Me too."

"Do you remember last night, Liz."

"Of course, John."

"I held you in my arms. It was so beautiful."

"It was beautiful...

By the way how was the drive earlier today? It wasn't too much for you, was it?"

"The drive went well. I heard one of our favorite songs."

"Wonderful. What song?"

"The song was "Landslide" Stevie Nicks."

"Duh. I know Stevie sang our "Landslide".

"Sorry. I'm getting a little sleepy."

"Before you fall asleep I want you to know we will be together again; I have it on the highest authority."

"Good to know. Hey that guy at the motel office said you weren't feeling well and had to leave."

"Feeling much better here with you."

"Oh good."

"I love you John."

"And I you sweetheart; just a few z's and I'll be fit as a fiddle."

"Okay love, go to sleep."

*

The sun was just coming up when I awoke. Liz was not in the room. There was a letter on the nightstand. On the envelope was written "open at our park".

*

As I'm driving to our park I thought back on last night.

There was no denying the god awful reality of aging and dying.

I knew Liz was dead.

*   *

"Hey Liz, sleepy head; we're almost there."

"The park?"

"Where else. Do you want a coffee.?"

"Is the Pope catholic."

"I still think that's funny."

"You would hon and that is why I love you."

"I think the coffee is cool enough to drink."

"It is, thanks. Oh what a beautiful day John."

"It is Liz.

"The clouds are so majestic!"

"A day fit for a Queen."

"Thank you, kind sir."

"Your welcome, me Lady."

"Such a beautiful park and no one here."

"How sad."

"Noooooooo John! How great. You can 'feel me up' without worrying about any one seeing."

"Oh Liz."

"Damn. You are blushing John."

"I am not."

"You are too."

"Not."

"Too x infinity."

"You always beat me to that."

"I do don't I?"

"There is the picnic table and benches."

"Newly painted."

"A forest green, Liz. How cool is that."

"Very."

I opened the picnic basket.

"You make the best egg and ham sandwich on a hard roll ever!"

"Thank you, love."

"You are welcome my dear."

"So what do you have there John?"

"It's not a 'Dear John" letter, is it Liz?"

"Well your name is John and it is a letter so yes it's a 'Dear John' letter; but one you saw coming. I wrote it last night."

"I see. You are always the mystery girl."

"Gotta keep up appearances and keep them guessing."

"One of the things I love about you."

"That's my guy."

"Stop staring. I will open the letter."

*

Dear John

I know you are reading this and I love communicating with you.

I ask you not to be sad. Considering my illness I'm in a better place.

Forgive me for coming back to you.

I wanted you to know that over the years the pain of leaving you never subsided. I should have given more consideration to adopting children and *not doing so is my ultimate regret.*

Do you remember the number of conversations we had regarding other-worldly stuff; angels, demons, ghosts, afterlife, parapsychology and astral projection?

I never did lose interest.

I got you to the motel. Love.

I got you to sleep off that 'little drunk'."

There are no arrangements.

I was born. I lived and loved. I died and will be remembered by family and friends until they die and then the remembering will be over.

A friend will take my ashes to this lake some early morning.

Remember I have our being together again on the Highest authority.

Good night my Love.

Always,

Liz

*

It was a quiet drive home. I did not turn on the radio.

I spent the day...I don't remember how I spent the day.

It is just as well.

I went to sleep that night in heavenly anticipation of not waking.

Alone In Car

My beloved wife Bette had been ill for the past year. She was hospitalized three times with the third being her last.

*

"I don't need to hon. I'm sure to feel warm soon."

"Bette, please. We have to go to the hospital. The doctor said he doesn't like your feeling such a chill and the blankets not helping. He's concerned about anemia."

"John. I'm afraid I won't come home."

*

Bette put up an amazing fight. At 4' 10" she was quite the lightweight in body but a heavy weight in spirit. I'm proud, numb and grief stricken; to think she would not say goodbye without undergoing multiple organ failure.

Bette's spirit left with nothing but praise for her body's 64 years.

She was conscious to the very last.

I was by her side when she left our world, my world, her world and found peace in the spiritual realm.

Hearing her last breath took mine away.

I must admit, as she lay dying, one of the dominant thoughts in my mind was her consistently saying over the past year...

"I'm not going anywhere honey; I'll forever be the bane of your existence."

I believed her.

Love's fool was I.

Our years together have been a time of love, laughter and the rare argument.

Unable to have children we accepted that as God's Will.

We did some fulfilling travel.

*

"John do you remember Mil and Harry?"

"Of course love. The elderly couple in New Hampshire's White Mountains."

"Yes and they showed us the photo of their deceased son."

"Oh God. He looked just like me."

"I know. And the four of us went on and on discussing reincarnation."

"Sad, huh?"

"It was John."

*

We made good friends.

We relished discovering the uniqueness of each other.

We loved living in New England. Bette loved the Summer and to be polite did not care for the Winter.

The interests we shared broadened each of our

horizons. Her love of Doo Wop and Motown...

*

"I went crazy with excitement when I got my first transistor radio. Oh how I listened to that music every chance I got."

*

...and my love of Classical and Musicals...

*

"When I brought over my CD of Sondheim's "Company" and you couldn't get enough of it...every time there was a nearby production you got tickets."

"And telling me he wrote Mom's and mine favorite song "Send in the Clowns" sealed my love for Mr. Sondheim."

*

...made for an evening of varied music that had us touting the richness of each piece played.

My interest in crime novels is thanks to her and

I'm sure to start reading one of her favorites sometime soon.

I wasn't much for travel but Bette's love of travel was contagious.

We bought the car we called 'black beauty' for our road trip to Miami.

We teased each other during the 3,000 mile round trip with quips about the next 100 miles being the 'deal breaker' (regarding our relationship) if either one of us says or does the wrong thing.

After the trip we bought a bottle of champagne to toast our 'successful bonding'.

When going away on a three day weekend in New England, which we did often, I would compile a list of esoteric subjects to discuss and after a few miles into the trip I would place the list in her waiting hand.

"Oh no the list!"

"Ah is my captive audience ready?"

"And willing but on one condition."

"I thought our love is unconditional?"

"Yes of course but with conditions."

"I'm sorry. I don't understand."

"Don't worry; you will in time. The condition is; when I say 'uncle' you stop talking."

"But what if I'm only half a dozen words in?"

"It's called trust hon. You're not saying you don't...

"No. Never."

I was able to discuss four subjects out of the list of seven; the price of unconditional love.

*

When Bette and I first met I would tease with...

"get to know me and I will tell you the meaning of life"

...she laughed saying she loved the mystery of that.

Over the years especially after a drink she would say 'oh by the way regarding the meaning of life I'm still waiting.'

The running gag is now over and the perilous thought of Bette's corporeal passing rendering the punchline worthless frightens me.

She was scared. I was scared. We didn't want to face the seriousness of Bette's illness. We left that to the health care people.

Our job was to remain hopeful, keep anxiety levels minimal and depression at bay.

We didn't talk about dying. Optimism ruled the day. Having more time together was the only course of action.

We dealt with the few close calls by my being a 'lovable jerk'; Bette's words.

*

I would search the hospital room.

"Nope not here. Closet empty. Nothing in the

drawers, just clothes. Bathroom; nothing but bathroom items. Nothing behind the blinds. No things swept under the carpet. Under the bed is clear."

And coming back to Bette, all smiles and breathing heavy would say,

"no ticket to be punched."

*

I believe the thought of dying was on her mind but Bette didn't broach the subject; wanting to protect me was of paramount concern.

In the end my Bette did not keep death waiting. She threw in the towel and rightly so; why sustain a few more punches when the judge has already decided.

She lost consciousness and passed away within twenty four hours.

Bette passed away at 1:05 AM.

The drive home from the hospital was a

mystery of survival.

How could I look at everything familiar to us with my eyes only.

And then coming home to our feline girls Enya and Tammy with their looking behind me for Bette...

They know she is gone and I wish I could comfort them.

The mornings are tough; waking to a new day holds little promise for renewal.

I am retired so I don't have to be at work.

Getting out of bed just to eat holds minimal appeal.

When I do get up there is no anticipation of engaging in anything meaningful.

I go hungry for a day or two and maybe a one-time favorite sandwich, tuna melt, will beckon.

Bette got a kick out of my taking the top layer of bread off the sandwich and cutting into it as one would an open face sandwich.

She always gave me her dill pickle; what a sweetheart.

After a few weeks with the loss of Bette I got it into my head to read books about grief.

The readings did not bring comfort.

Reading about grief may be akin to finding the enemy's war plans and discovering their strategy for taking you down.

Grief has invaded every molecule of my body.

Grief occupies every brain neuron.

Grief has taken away my search for meaning.

When I momentarily forget she is gone and think of sharing something with Bette the forgetting becomes a sledgehammer and the once solid edifice of self crumbles under the blow.

I do believe I'm living a dual existence. The one life is about Bette and all memory of her. The other life is the loss of Bette and the black hole with attending defeat in the game of life.

I don't go out much and a good part of that is not wanting to be alone in the car.

*

The time of this writing is late July, an early morning. It is three months since Bette passed away.

I went to the grocery store and again walked by the foods Bette and I enjoyed; with her being gone they have no appeal.

I didn't have to get much, a half-gallon of milk some cans of soup and food for Enya and Tammy.

I put the grocery bag on the back seat. I leave the passenger seat alone.

I am home in the car. Our parking space faces a wooded area. We liked that being the last thing we see when we get out of the car.

I'm still in the car. I don't want to move.

Through the front windshield I look at the trees

where a few leaves are turning color.

I close my eyes.

"John honey do you believe there are a few leaves starting to turn and it's only late July."

"I know sweetheart-we have to report this-who do we report this to Bette?"

"I don't know John-aren't you the guy who knows the meaning of life-you should have some idea of who to contact."

"Okay I know. I'll make a call."

"To who?"

"God."

"Why?"

"God is the One Who gives it all meaning."

Silence.

"You didn't say anything."

"No answer."

"Try again, love."

"I will later, sweetheart."

"Okay just as long you keep trying."

Dear Bette

This is my first letter since you passed away, Love. Every previous attempt met with profound sadness robbing me of any coherent thought. I'm sorry it took awhile.

After a time I started what I call my "Grief Journal".

I guess you can think of the journal entries as letters of a sort but they are without the "Dear Bette" and it does make a difference; I'm not sure why.

I am comforted knowing my words will reach you.

It's hard to say where my mind is at. I walk in a fog. I am numb. I am prone to staring at a fixed object for a long time. I am incredibly sad. I am without desire, interest and can no longer recollect that damn 'meaning of life' we talked about or I should say I teased you about.

God has been silent.

Or

I am deaf.

The other night there was a storm; you would have loved it.

Before falling asleep I thought back to my youth and being at camp. I don't know where that came from but there it was. The memory of feeling homesick swept over me. I remember writing a letter to Mom and feeling a connection to her and less homesick in the writing.

I wanted to be brave and I think the words betrayed that a little but I continued writing. I thought of my emotional survival as being dependent on the writing. The letter got me trough the night with the day bringing activity and fun. In less then twenty four hours I grew accustomed to the place.

How I wish writing my letter to you would offer a bit of that solace.

So I fell asleep knowing the place of mourning, where I am at now will suffer no acclimation.

Grief will not be appeased.

I am compelled to write the letter anyway.

Are you behind that?

My words are scattered thoughts begging for cohesion. They ache for a narrative captivating enough to rock your world. I can't think of them as futile attempts to connect. I can't. It is unacceptable.

I miss you. I think of our life together and all the fun we had asking the questions and looking for the answers.

I try to give the memories a consoling nostalgic spin but the remembering hurts too much. When I say hurt I mean it is...

...stop what I'm doing, sit down before the lightheadedness causes me to lose balance and I reach for your hand that is not there.

I know my heart can withstand only so many breaks before it surrenders but it will not.

As long as there is memory of you my heart will go on beating.

The strength of your memory sustains me and I

am grateful.

Every time I bring you to the forefront of my mind my eyes well up and you know the rest...

I wonder about your new life. Does the LOVE that surrounds you allow for memory of our Love.

I would like to believe 'yes' but that would be selfish of me.

Is it fair that I ask you to remember me?

There should be no room for my grief in your world.

How can I let my grief touch you.

I can't.

Let the letter come back with 'return to sender- no forwarding address'.

I would be happy with that.

But what if the letter isn't returned and how do I interpret that?

Is there a part of you that lets in the world left behind?

What in our life can compare to what you are experiencing now in you new life?

Isn't our Love only a faint reflection of what you have before you?

Might it be better if the 'higher ups' impose a clean break of things?

Then it would only be fair the 'clean break' applies to me.

And

Grief is no more.

Am I writing myself out of a correspondence with you?

I shall quit this line of inquiry while I am ahead.

*

Not much has changed on the physical landscape.

I haven't moved to another home; how could I?

Enya and Tammy are with me. They mean so much to us.

I'm still retired.

I don't drink alcohol any longer.

I sleep or doze off more than ever.

The apartment is as it was and the view through the bedroom window has not altered.

*

What has changed is everything else.

What has changed is the effort it takes to wake with the sun, to get through a day, to find motivation, to feel good about being alive...

I think of my heart as an empty chamber echoing with spoken words of love.

I want the present words to take flight and find you.

I want you in my arms again and for you to know I will always love you.

*

Enya, Tammy and I had a talk one night, not long ago, (well I did the talking) about Mommy being gone.

I love them dearly and for their sake wish Mommy was here and Daddy gone.

Enya walks by your recliner and she stops for a moment to look up to see if you are there, then continues walking.

Tammy lies on your bed pillow at night.

When I come home they stand at the front door waiting for you to follow.

How they love you.

*

Last night I dreamed you came home. I started shaking when I saw you and not in fear, of course but in euphoria.

You were healthy. The smile and mischievous look in your eyes was glad to find me surprised.

I stood there thinking my heart is going to stop due to unfathomable happiness. I let out a shout for joy and then you were gone. I woke up in tears.

How can a dream be so cruel?

*

How am I going to get there, hon. I don't even know where there is for God's sake. And if there is a there I know I'm not anywhere near it.

*

Hurting Times.

The kitchen was the first room you saw when you found the apartment. I was at work and you call me saying the worker is doing finishing touches on the cabinet and no you are not bothering him as you peer through the patio glass door smiling and he smiles back.

I said yes that day to the place on your assessment and it's been home ever since.

I do sit at the kitchen table after having put together a quick meal and I am willing to deal with the pain of missing you.

Why?

For the delight of humorous kitchen memories.

I'm at the sink and you sneak up behind me...'Boo'.

You got Motown blasting and hips a be-bopping.

At the table, late at night, the bottle of wine between us-gone and you say 'Now god-damn it! What is the meaning of life?' I am about to speak and you say 'Oh never mind, I'm tired. You can tell me in the morning.'

*

How do I continue to look out on the patio from the living room love seat and see the empty space once occupied by a table and chair where you, on a summer evening, would either read, check in with Facebook or deign to speak with me if I happened to be more interesting.

I do try to find solace in the memory of being there with you.

It is a warm evening and the clouds are picking up a tinge of pink from the setting sun. The 'Mastress' chef is at the grill with swordfish a cooking, hips a swinging to the "Jersey Boys" musical and a smile that sends me to the warmest place in my heart.

It is difficult to look at the sky and not remember our silly game of watching, from the patio, for Bradley or Logan bound airlines and keeping track of who sees the plane first and whoever reaches 10 first wins.

And when it comes to the sky, oh how you would say "Promises, promises" after hearing the forecast for a storm and smiling at me knowing full well that at the first hint of thunder and lightening I am under the covers.

*

The other day I was in the library looking for a movie to borrow and I realized the ones I watched with you will never be seen again. And that is how it should be.

You loved the "islands" as a young woman and soon after we met said we have to go. We never went and I will never go. And that is how it should be.

There are restaurants we frequented and I will never go back. And that is how it should be.

There are songs we danced to and I will never dance to them again. And that is how it should be.

There are songs we loved and I can't listen to again. And that is how it should be.

There are TV shows we liked and to watch them would only have me looking at the recliner from my chair with immeasurable sadness; so I don't watch them. And that is how it should be.

*

I don't think we talked enough about death, hon.

I know you ask what difference it would have made and I guess I agree.

And you could say we said everything there was to say in the course of our relationship.

I'm not sure.

I don't men to suggest talking would have provided any kind of emotional preparation for either of us dying but maybe just maybe a comforting idea might have come up between us.

I'm left now to consider this alone and I don't mean to imply any fault on your part.

I believe the little we did talk of death and grief was typical in its brevity and desire not to 'go there' because we gotta lot of living to do.

So I ask.

If we had given death and grief a more thorough gander could we have come up with a spell maybe even a potion I could now take and be less stricken?

You know the Polish 'witch' in you I loved also scared the hell out of me.

I like to think if we knew then what I know now we would have been desperate to come up with something that would keep grief from making desperate the state of my soul.

I suspect this is called 'magical thinking'.

*

I know you'd rather not read this love but the sad truth is all my senses are diminished since you been gone.

The crater in my being left by your loss is incredible.

*

Okay. Okay. Okay. I know.

Yes I am alive.

And it is good for Enya, Tammy and folks who care about me.

And.

Yes I remember us and all we were and are to each other.

And.

I do take comfort in that; no matter the pain.

*

I know we can't hold back the tide of time.

Yet it is maddening when holding onto one another with all the loving strength we have

And still the tide tears us apart.

*

On any given day I'm sad and angry. The two emotions are coexisting. They dominate my life.

I am sad because I can not touch you and talk to you and make you laugh.

I am angry because I can not touch you and talk to you and make you laugh.

In spite of the pain I can not tolerate the thought of Grief leaving my side.

Grief is the last profound connection between

us.

It is the emotion that profoundly tells me you were here and loved.

As you dear heart remain absent from this corporeal world I will countenance that absence with Love and anguish.

Truly Yours

John

Love Letter

Okay. Okay. Okay. I know.

And no I am not going bonkers. I am only Eighty One for Pete's sake.

And I don't know who the hell Pete is.

I have time on my hands and what better way to spend it than to write you a love letter.

And I know it's sweet. It is damn sweet.

And my Nurse Sarah tells me it's sweet.

But.

Honestly Love I don't want sweet I want you.

And yes I know you are not here to write me a sweet love letter in response.

But

You know what?

"What John"

You say you are not here but I know different.

Yeah. Yeah. Yeah. I have that covered.

I will write your love letter to me.

And yes it will be all love dovey because I know you girls like lovey dovey.

And I want to do everything you like.

And...

Let me remind you how many times you asked me to tell you why you love me; well here you go and it will be in writing.

Oh, one more thing. I will bring up how we met on the psychiatric ward and the Nurse 'ethics' thing. I'm sure you won't mind.

It says a lot about our Love and the extraordinary person you are.

And Fate.

The love letter will be written by the younger me on the psychiatric ward.

I will start now my Love.

*

This is my love letter. I believe we have the real thing; the real glorious thing.

I am writing to a smart, compassionate, beautiful woman.

And I hardly know you.

I only met you a month ago.

You have chosen the Psychiatric Nursing profession where you shine and the men and women on the edge of darkness are welcoming of your light.

Their vulnerability is no less sacred than the anesthetized patient under the surgeon's scalpel.

You honor and respect the patients and bring a profound compassion to their care. Your kindness and reassurance starts them on the road to recovery.

Your asking me to write a Journal was a good idea; window to the soul and all that stuff.

I have discovered things about myself I'm not sure I would have if not for the journaling and the conversations with you afterward. I treasure the insight and humor you provide.

I sincerely appreciate your helping me gain confidence and self-awareness.

I have to tell you that your questions, listening, and eye contact communicate to me that I truly matter.

Sometimes for us mentally ill the 'matter' thing comes under question.

I hope I'm not being a downer.

I'm going to sound like someone from personnel now...

"Miss Bette, the continuing education you pursue to enhance the quality of patient care is very admirable."

I hope when I continue my education I'm able to bring such diligence and fortitude to bear on my studies.

What I love to meditate over is the naturalness you bring to it all.

I marvel at your intuition.

Your 'gut feeling' never seems to let you down.

How impressive in getting to the heart of the matter.

Everything has its 'ideal' and for Psychiatric Nursing it is you.

*

Should I say how selfish of me to expect anything from you other than your professionalism as a Nurse which is irreproachable.

*

As we know I am schizophrenic and I will be the rest of my life. What kind of catch am I? Ball game over. I will take my glove, ball, bat and go home.

But

I want to play. And now that I have met you I need to play.

I keep coming around to the mental illness as the barrier to our love. I know you wouldn't see it that way.

But still...

It is suggested one doesn't bring work home and here you are (possibly) coming home to 'your work'.

I suspect you would say that is terribly

unfair on my part; after all Love is a two way street.

I know, I know and anxiously wait to hear from you.

I find my Obsessive Compulsive Disorder scarier than the Schizophrenia; sounds crazy, huh?

I think it is the intellectual awareness of the crippling OCD and not many resources to do anything about it.

Whereas the Schizophrenia is responding to the medication.

It is all the more exacerbating because even with you by my side I could still find it hard to get through a particular OCD episode; like having a strong arm to hold me steady and I still lose balance.

Damn, that is frustrating.

I want you to know I believe it is natural that I think about you and your quality of life in relation to my mental illness. I want the best for you.

You know I love you and if you love me it...may not be enough.

I must take courage from you and consider myself worthy in spite of the mental illness.

It worries me; as a society we don't care for our mentally ill as well as the physically ill.

I know in understanding the mind   there is a lot of 'grey' area.

And...

...let us not forget mental illness harbors behavior that may offend.

And...

...physical illness harbors behavior that may elicit sympathy.

*

Can love abide a failure of nature? Here's hoping.

What is my gallery status? Am I worthy of a viewing?

Am I feeling sorry for myself? Probably.

Sorry for going on...supposed to be a love letter not a self-pity letter.

I should try to keep the feeling sorry for myself at bay; right?

"Right."

Thanks. I needed that.

*

Your light touch with the application of your perfume is lovely and did you know in that light touch you may be allowing your pheromone's to capture the olfactory me and they say that's a good start.

Hey, I'm not sure if I told you I am a virgin. There it is; I am.

"That wasn't so bad."

My parents did a good job of emphasizing love over lust.

What I want to believe is the waiting is the knowing you were out there.

And that is what I will believe.

The reincarnation thing has always fascinated me. When you think about it, finding your soulmate is reuniting with the Love that has been far away.

*

Do you mind if I say I'd be remiss in not letting you in on the humor that is in me.

Wanna hear a dirty joke? A white horse fell in the mud.

The intellect I nurture; Plato is more than stretchy doh.

The love of the Arts; a great reason to live in a metropolis.

And the immense curiosity for life; from the farms of ants to the galaxy of stars.

I hope you have a liking for adventure. To explore the sights, smells and sounds of our natural and urban wilderness with you would give me such joy.

I yearn to gather understanding of our

complexities.

I want to work on the puzzle of life with no picture and pieces falling from the sky.

I want to get inside your head.

I want to know everything there is to know about you.

But

I appreciate and respect the need for you to keep secrets.

What's that you say.

You may ask why there are secrets between two people very much in love...

...here's hoping about the very much in love part.

I will tell you about secrets.

They say there ought to be a 'wisp of mystery' to keep the flame alive in a relationship.

I'm not sure one can be mysterious without being secretive.

When I say mysterious I don't mean anything nefarious. I mean innocent, innocuous; like how do you keep that eye brow upturned for so long, why do I sing the same aria in the shower, what did you to do to your best friend Cathy when you were five and she wouldn't talk to you for a week (Cathy didn't say what happened), and what did I do as an altar boy during Mass that had the congregation in 'stitches'.

You know, those kinds of things.

*

When it comes to writing in my journal the true experience of me is lost in translation.

The intricacies of our minds ask for delicate probing that only shared time and conversation can provide.

To imagine where our Love can take us fills me with joy:

The glorious summer day we hike up Mt. Washington in New Hampshire and enjoy the summit view and when we are spiritually rejuvenated we start our descent that leads us to deer on the trail waiting to be seen by us.

The Puccini aria that has us in tears at the Metropolitan Opera House New York City and next day in the New York Times the music critic speculates it was sung by the 'tenor of the decade'.

The club dancing where years into our relationship we are surrounded by beautiful people and no one tempts our eyes to stray because the honeymoon is not over.

The day with friends when 'Love is all we need' is the communal mantra.

The afternoon at Riverside Park in Manhattan where the flowers share their colors and scents with lovers passing by.

And the ocean cruise where we leave our cabin late at night and are enveloped by the Stygian sky and sea complementing the decadent revelry of earlier partying or as one might say 'a hell of a party'.

I can't wait to learn about you.

You have shared a little and I thank you for that. I know the reluctance has to do with patient/therapist ethics.

Every fiber of my being wants us to be a couple and so I dream.

I dream of being in the home you grew up in and sitting on the living room couch side by side and looking at every photo ever taken of you even the goofy ones.

I dream of our walking your neighborhood where you went to elementary and high school and hung out with friends.

I dream of our spending a weekend at your college and walking the campus while you regale me with stories especially the embarrassing ones.

I dream of showing you my college stomping grounds and having a drink in the bar where I read my Dostoevsky.

I dream of attending sporting events and cheering our team on with friends.

I dream of incredible conversations following the play-the movie-the book-the opera-

the concert-the exhibit at the museum-the college lecture-the political event and the favorite television drama.

I dream of a minor physical illness I contract that commands your full attention maybe even to feeding me ice cream.

I dream of alternate chapter readings of Charles Dickens "David Copperfield" and letting his world enter ours to the delight of our love and sense of social justice.

I dream of the church we call a second home where His Love and Grace help us make some sense of it all.

I dream of the carousel where we sit together in the carriage and our love melding in the centrifugal force.

I dream of being in bed with our hands

clasped by our side, the sun rising above the trees outside our bedroom window and the smell of coffee brewing and we are eager to make it a memorable day.

I dream of dinner prep time spent in the kitchen with the result being your utmost appreciation for the pasta meal I prepare and I removing your sauce stained white T-shirt that I promptly place in the clothes hamper and get you a red T-shirt that I pull down over your head with smiles that become kisses on the neck...

And I dream of dying in your arms and taking my love for you into eternity.

I hope you understand I must die first because to live without you is not an option. And I'm sorry for that.

You know when they talk about love and

the couple being as one is 'devoutly to be wished for'; well how glorious is that?

But (here I go again)

I believe the precious sentiment can compromise the expression of our true self.

Oh, okay I know...

'What the hell do you mean by that?'

I know it sounds strange.

'Duh'

But

'Watch out he's getting preachy'

We can not assume our love for a book, a movie, a painting etc. will win her or him 'over' to the same appreciation.

If we are bummed because our loved one

doesn't share the same feeling for a film we must celebrate the difference.

I know couples would have a better time of it with the realization that what rocks my world will not necessarily rock yours.

When it comes to an appreciation for a work of Art a candid dissenting opinion by the loved other could easily let you in on their diversity of thought.

That being said Bette,

I can't imagine our not appreciating a lot of the same things by virtue of falling in love and finding one another compatible.

What do you think?

I can't wait for your answer!

Bette, Sweetheart I think of you to

distraction and I hope you don't find fault in that.

I made a list (I do have time on my hands, after all) and it is by no means complete but let it suffice as a way of communicating my interests.

I understand that interests would normally come up over the course of having dialogues and monologues in a 'normal courtship' but I haven't had that luxury.

So taking pen to journal I imagine being by your side and wondering...

Wondering about your interests and passions.

And I will tell you of mine.

I wonder about your love of:

Literature (novel-novella-short story-play-poem), nonfiction (biographies, autobiographies, memoirs, history, commentary, essay, cultural pieces).

My top five writers (Fyodor Dostoevsky-Charles Dickens-Hermann Hesse-Ernest Hemingway-John Irving).

Music (symphony-tone poem-concerto-chamber-opera-oratorio-mass-rock n'roll-country-jazz-folk-film score, musical).

My top five classical composers (Vivaldi-Mozart-Beethoven-Wagner-Mahler-Aaron Copland-sorry couldn't do five).

My top five film composers (John Barry-John Williams-Georges-Delarue-Rachel Portman-Max Richter).

Paintings (cave art-landscape-portrait-still life-baroque-renaissance-impressionism-modern, abstract).

My top five painters (Leonardo Da Vinci-Van Gogh-Monet-Renoir-Edward Hopper).

And

Politics, cultural mores, architecture, fashion design, yoga, meditation, ballet, modern dance, theater, cinema, sculpture, documentaries

Radio (news-music-talk)

Television (drama-sitcom-talk-food-news-soap operas-sports)

Sports (baseball-football-basketball-soccer-softball-tennis-golf-hockey, lacrosse)

Tree climbing, camping, hiking, rock climbing, roller skating, skiing, ice skating, skate boarding, deep sea diving, snorkeling, surfing

Transportation

Cars (sports-convertible-color-speed)

Trucks, bus, cab, subway, train, airplane, cruise,

And

Mountains, oceans, glaciers, lakes, rivers, canyons, deserts, forests

Foods I'd have to be really nuts to go individual foods

Okay just a couple

Ice cream, pizza---I couldn't help myself

Restaurants, gossip, celebrity gossip

Top ten cities I have visited or would like to visit   (Boston-Washington   D.C.-Chicago-Los Angeles-New York -Dublin-Paris-Prague-Peking-Sydney).

Top ten countries I would like to visit (Ireland-England-Italy-France-Spain   -Sweden-

Germany-Russia-India-Greece   -South Korea), (sorry 11).

Top five last things to do with a week to live:

Hold you in my arms and talk about reincarnation and coming back to you.

Hold you in my arms and talk about the hereafter.

Hold you in my arms and talk about the cosmos.

Hold you in my arms and talk about the abundance of joy we gave each other in the time we had.

Hold you in my arms and know our spirits will always be together.

The letter you are reading is my beacon of

light; hoping the ray catches you.

It is my fervent desire for you to see the whole of me and not just the patient.

My mental illness be damned.

I have enough insight and intuitiveness regarding you.

The label 'transference' does not apply.

You know that my love for you is real.

It is not a vulnerable soul looking for a savior. It is not gratitude substituting for love.

It is what happened when we met and I saw you for the angel that you are.

And

Quantum physics had to be a part of it; our waves of subatomic particles crested on each other's shore and immediately knew after traveling the sea of energy-they were home.

I dream of making love to you and we become one with the universe...

And are given a deeper love for all life.

*

As I'm sure you can imagine the wrap up to The Love Letter has been the assignment of all assignments and I fear to disappoint.

I like to keep things simple when I can and I thought of two parallel trails in the forest about to converge.

You are walking one and I the other.

We meet.

The sun breaks through the clouds.

The sun's rays through the canopy of trees find us and we are illuminated.

Far Away *John Crawford*

I love you, Bette

Sincerely,

Forever yours,

John

Far Away *John Crawford*

Love Letter

How strange to be writing your love letter to me. I like that it allows me the opportunity to get into your head.

I will admit to writing down all I have heard you say at one time or another.

And

I will admit to writing all I have heard you not say and hope it was just a matter of time before you said it.

The love letter is being written by the younger you.

Let the Love Letter begin.

Dear John

I have waited for this day like no other day in my life when I write the love letter of my dreams.

Your subtle and sometimes not so subtle courtship in your Journal thrilled me in ways the teen in me giggled and the adult approved.

I know I have met my soul mate.

I live with a friend named Pauline who is a medical nurse at New York-Presbyterian Hospital. I told her about you and after a couple weeks confided in her my anxiety over feelings for you. She is supportive. We talked about the ethics and she said 'in matters of the heart don't mess with destiny'.

Her words resonated.

The past month when I arrive at work and before getting out of the car I open my planner to verify the number of days before your discharge and vow to stay cool.

I'm sure you understand that violating a

cardinal rule of Nursing was bound to weigh heavy on my mind.

The 'rule' asked my heart to be still.

At times in reading your Journal I would get emotional and need to hold the book away from me for fear of it catching a tear drop.

While reading your words I would hear your voice...

(by the way, my love, you have a very sexy voice)

...in my mind and it took me to a place a therapist should not go with their patient.

I knew then I was in trouble. Any reference of love you made in the journal had me in a panic.

Because...

I felt the same way.

I started to feel guilty for not reciprocating your love and leaving you out in the cold, so to speak.

I am sorry.

*

I will have you know that I also believe there was something about us from the very beginning.

When I first saw you on the ward tied to a gurney my heart broke.

And then having to stick you with the needle to administer the sedative; I saw myself through your eyes as some bad gal in a movie.

Later I smiled to myself hoping you wouldn't be mad at me.

*

While relaying your fears and anxieties during our talks with candor and vulnerability it was difficult not to reach out for your hand.

At times I would look out the window from the ward and see you alone on the bench. I admire your willingness to be alone. I know that is who you are. I share that trait.

We both know there is space on the bench for another and I hope to occupy that space dear John.

By the way how diabolical of you to court me with your Journal. Talk about a captive audience.

I have to tell you that no girl should be held back on going head over heels for their love. I will give kismet a 'what for'.

The Journal pages where you prepare a

scramble egg breakfast I gladly insert myself as the recipient.

I then take it further and imagine that breakfast as the start of the perfect weekend.

After the kitchen clean-up we make love again; for we had done so upon waking.

We both dress in sneakers, blue jeans and T-shirts. My T-shirt is "Greenpeace" and yours is "Habitat for Humanity".

We leave the apartment and walk up the street to Mrs. Rivera's grocery store for some trail mix. She asks us to join her for coffee and we do. We tell her we will be back tomorrow for groceries.

The meandering route to the book store allows us to check out architectural highlights of the neighborhood.

At the bookstore I buy John Irving's latest

and a Modern Library edition of Dicken's "David Copperfield".

We know the owner and his name is Mandy. I eventually hope to stop him from insisting I quit nursing and head to Hollywood to be the starlet I'm meant to be.

The day continues to be beautiful, bright and warm.

You convince me, against my better nutritional judgment, to have a hot dog with all the fixings.

Lincoln Center is just across the street.

The schedule of events for the theaters at Lincoln Center are available and we round them up to peruse while sitting on a bench in Lincoln Center's Damrosch Park eating our hot dogs.

The performances we agree upon give us

*concerts, operas and ballets to look forward to for
the fall and winter.*

*In your hometown of Park Slope, Brooklyn
we walk Prospect Park. I love all the childhood
stories you regale me with especially the bicycle
riding and racing.*

*We go to your childhood home; your
parents are not there and what a mischievous boy
you are when you get me into your bedroom.*

*After walking across the Brooklyn Bridge
and picking up the "Village Voice" we find an ad for
a mini Bergman film festival.*

*We loved "Autumn Sonata". The plot
dealing with an aloof mother and estranged adult
daughter was foreign to us but we ask questions of
each other to elicit observations and insights that
enrich our relationship.*

The next day is Sunday paper and old movies on TV.

Later in the day we go to the grocery store and Mrs. Rivera is happy to see us.

We pick up several items to make a salad for dinner.

We are in the kitchen and I ask to help.

You say: "We are having pasta; do you know how to boil water?"

I shoot you a glance that drops you to the floor.

We put together the shell pasta dinner with Newman's sauce and the Italian bread is fresh. We enjoy red wine while we talk about our fun filled day and how exhausted we are.

Later, on the couch drinking coffee we talk

about the second perfect weekend and what it will entail:

That little extra of Irish butter brings my scrambled eggs first to the finish line.

Buying a colorful sweater for each other at Macy's.

Standing in line at TKTS in Times Square and hoping a pair of tickets is available for the matinee show we are most interested in.

A couple hours at the Guggenheim Museum; there's a Parrish there I love.

The Central Park Carousel .

Dinner with your parents. We have dinner at the Water's Edge in Long Island City, Queens. The food is incredible.

On Sunday we gather food items for our

picnic basket from Mrs. Rivera's grocery store.

We drive up to Tanglewood where we will hear Mahler's Resurrection Symphony.

We sit on a World Wildlife Fund blanket with a panda bear motif, enjoying our little picnic.

Later we enjoy dinner; you and your salmon, me and my scallops.

We stay at a nearby motel.

The love making is memorable being both athletic and artistic.

Our paths have merged and our journey will be traveled as one.

I look forward to numerous intellectual and sport competitions with the loser buying jewelry of my choice.

You know that feeling of things going so

well it could not get better.

It's a beautiful sentiment but by virtue of loving me your reality of 'things going so well' truly won't get better and sadly, for you.

You will not get better than me in chess, tennis, poker, command of witticism, rhymes smack down, accurate interpretation of Shakespeare , singing Stephen Sondheim's "Getting Married Today" and not missing one word...

And

...my fourth grade understanding of Quantum Physics beats your twelfth grade understanding of Quantum Physics.

So how does it feel to have met your better half?

Speaking of getting married, we will know when the time is right. We will think of our declaration of love as the prelude to marriage.

Latin for prelude is 'play before'. Do you find that curious?

I don't want to imply in any way, no matter what the cynics say, that marriage is the end of play.

Our marriage will be the beginning of serious play and joy; bringing a baby into the world!

In the meanwhile we work and play hard.

We love our family and friends.

We will treasure the backyard barbecue where everybody catches up to what's been going on among us and then let the talk branch out to politics, religion, the Arts, culture, gossip, etc....

We will travel roads of compassion and

help those who have lost their way.

We will partake of conversations where the vicissitudes of life we countenance demand careful attention and by that attention we are better able to mature in spirit and empathize with others.

Our journey will be one of profound love for each other.

Our journey will be one of caring for others.

*

Yesterday morning I woke up suddenly from a dream. I dreamt we were married and upon waking, in the dream, I turned toward you and felt such a heart stopping loss in not seeing you. The dream was amazingly vivid. I was shaken and started to cry.

I worry you may give up on me. I worry you may misinterpret my behavior. I worry you will leave the hospital. I wouldn't blame you.

I am so grateful for your courage in reaching out to me and shouldering the risk of being rejected. I hope I didn't make it too difficult for you.

*

My dearest John, I will always love you and let vibrant and joyful colors grace the canvas of our life.

Let our painting be in the gallery of eternal love.

My deep love for you has opened a new world for me; one seen through your eyes. I accept that as a wonderful gift.

I am strong and independent; my love and passion for you says to me there is a chance a wonderful chance that our lives together will be of love, peace, kindness and empathy in a world of abject cruelty and sublime joy.

Our Witness as a couple will have begun.

I am beside myself in anticipation of how much delirious fun awaits us as a twosome and don't forget to fasten your seatbelt, honey. I will always love you.

Yours Forever,

Love

Bette

Bette's Old Guy

John is in a nice nursing home. Every morning when he awakes he wonders how much longer he will be in the nursing home.

He has been without his adored wife Bette for awhile now. After Bette passed away life lost much of its flavor; ensuing years have made it a little more palatable.

The wonder of Bette is she truly loved John. He never thought much of his looks; as far as she was concerned he was a 'matinee idol'. He doubted his worth as a writer; as far as she was concerned his writing was very much worth the read. He worried his intellect would intimidate her; as far as she was concerned it only motivated her to outsmart him every chance she got.

His missing her has not diminished since the

day she passed away.

*

Sarah is an aide in the nursing home.

"How are you today Sarah?"

"I'm good John and you?"

"I am doing better, now that you are here.

"Ah the charmer."

"It's all I have left dear."

"More than enough John."

"You are so sweet. So what can you tell an eighty one year old guy about your plans for this evening that will make him jealous?"

"Let's see; dinner for the hubby and two kids, laundry and the bills. Jealous?" 111

"Yes as a matter of fact. I bet your dinner is

terrific."

"Thank you John. Though the meals here are good...Yes you can be jealous."

"Okay then so I have dibs on the leftovers?"

"Yes."

"Thanks Sarah, but, considering your meals being so good and all, will there be leftovers?"

"I will make sure."

" Oh thank you so much, my dear."

"You are welcome."

"Isn't it remarkable how in our later years food becomes quite the pleasure."

"I hear that a lot from the others."

"Nice day today Sarah."

"Yes and they say the rest of the week will be

nice too; no snow storms."

"That's good. Look at the way it's piling up out there; a few inches and the snow will be at the window sill."

"Of course the kids love it. They can't wait to go to the park and snow slide."

"How old?"

"Eight and ten."

"Oh yeah; good ages for that kind of fun. For Bette snow was the 'other' four letter word."

"That's funny."

"Yeah. Bette was not a snow bunny."

"You okay, John. You seem kind of tired."

"I am Sarah. I don't know why. Had a good night sleep except for that damn prostate, but I am used to that."

"Well... you take a nap whenever you want to."

"Okay. By the way how long have I been here at the nursing home?"

"A month, why?"

"Just wondering. Have I told you about Bette?"

"Yes, your wife; the two of you were very much in love."

"Yes we were and are. She is in the spirit world, you know. I haven't heard from her lately. No signs that I can pick up on, anyway. I wonder why. Do you think she is coming back Sarah; reincarnation and all that?"

Sarah took John's hand.

"Wouldn't that be something John."

"It would Sarah, it would."

"Would you like some tea and a biscuit with

strawberry jam?"

"My favorite, yes dear. Take your time, I'm not going anywhere."

*

John's sister Pat convinced him it was time to be in a home.

The fall and laying unconscious for the day got the conversation going.

She found a nice one in Cape Cod Massachusetts.

It was expensive but he could afford it thanks to Bette.

John grew up reading the Classics and rereading them through out his life.

After Bette's passing and retirement from social work he embarked on a writing journey. The waters he navigated were literary. The joke between him and Pat was; I been on this writer's craft for a few years now and the fish are not biting.

He self-published five books and sales amounted to less than a hundred.

Then one morning as he was in the kitchen sipping coffee and missing Bette, as always, the night's dream came to him.

Bette was on the writer's craft and a storm was brewing. It was hard to hear her above the wind.

'What's that hon? You want cereal?'

'No sweetheart you do.'

'I'm not hungry, though.'

'You want to create a serial killer.'

'Honey, who goes around killing cereal?'

'No sweetheart a serial killer; you know one

who kills more than one person.'

'Oh that's funny; here I've been writing about us, love, grief, compassion, empathy, fine arts, noble pursuits, nature, philosophical and theological subjects and you want me to write about a murderer?'

'Yes dear. You can make a killing, excuse the pun and believe me the fish will start biting.'

John was animated in the telling and when he stopped Sarah looked dubious.

"John you pulling my leg or did you really have that dream?"

"I really did have the dream Sarah and not just the one. I had two more within that same week with Bette providing a bit of the killer's profile and the one thing the killer does to elicit sympathy from the reader."

"I'm not into crime books but you got me interested so I'll have to read yours. Can you tell me anything more; like a 'trailer' to a movie?"

"Well dear I don't want to give away too much but let's see; the killer is self aware regarding his compulsion to kill and chooses bad guys for victims."

"Like a vigilante?"

"Kind of but it is more to assuage his guilt for killing them."

"I see."

"He sends a recording to the victim's family.

It is a recording of the victim's last words. He suggests children not be in earshot of the recording because of the vituperative language.

He does that because he doesn't want to be

seen in a bad light.

He has no regret.

He does ask the family to forgive the murdered one."

"A real sicko. I can't wait to read it. I'm going to buy the book and will you autograph it?"

"Of course. How about the literary ones?"

"Oh yes of course but first the killer, okay?"

"Sure."

"So the serial killer made you a lot of money?"

"Yes. And fortunately the literary books did better as a result of my killer's popularity. I give thanks to Bette. "

"She's watching out for you."

"She is Sarah. I got myself a heavenly muse.

You wanna hear something funny?"

"Please."

"A few people, here in the home, are reading me and have no idea I am among them."

John took notice of Sarah's puzzled look.

"The author's photo is me as a young man. The publisher said young authors sell better than old ones."

"That's interesting. I will have to keep an eye out. Would you like me to divulge your identity?"

"I have thought about it and prefer the anonymity."

"Well you let me know if you change your mind. I'm sure the ladies would love to know you are in their midst."

"Too kind... Bette's birthday is tomorrow."

"Is there anything special you'd like to do?"

"Can't think of anything. I know if I had more energy I'd say a drive to Provincetown. Bette and I loved visiting Provincetown. On some visits we did the 'bar crawl' along Commercial Street and oh the loving people we met; so much gaiety!"

"I bet."

"So I'll sit here and remember."

"Yes."

"I feel blessed that the memories haven't strayed too far away."

"Yes. Any more tea, John?"

"I'm good, thanks.'

"Just let me know."

"I will sweetheart."

"Good."

"Do you have a little more time for me Sarah."

"I'm not going anywhere."

"I am sadly remembering less of our road trip to Miami.

It was funny in that we secretly wondered if the trip from Middletown Connecticut to Miami Florida was going to make or break us.

Bette's mantra for the trip was 'Going to Miami' ; sung with a lilt in her voice.

I teased her..."

'...Honey the 100th time I hear 'Going to Miami' could be the deal breaker.'

"She laughed and retorted..."

'...Baby face your incessant talk and obsession with God, philosophy and determinism will become

the deal breaker.'

'Crumb cake I thought you loved me for my smarts?'

'Sweetie pie I do. It's just that I don't want to get fat on your intellect. It is all about portions.'

'Yes you are right.'

'Why don't you talk about sports?'

'I don't know much about sports.'

'I know.'

"I can still see her 4'10" beauty in the passenger seat with feet on the dashboard or out the window.

When she saw I was getting a little tired (I assured her I would pull over if I felt too tired) she would start to sing off key and move her upper body. Once in a while she would flash her...well you know but flash only to me."

"Ah John and naughty Bette."

"She was the naughty one, Sarah. I was the innocent bystander."

"I'm sure."

John looked out the window for a bit.

"Everything okay John?"

"The memories of Bette in the hospital are sketchy..."

"Tough memories John, maybe just as well?"

"You would think but I'd have to say no.

Loss of memory only adds to the grief of losing her.

I do remember her having a smile and kind word for all hospital personnel from Doctor to maintenance worker.

She had a round, cherub like face and her emerald eyes and smile kept you from leaving her presence anytime soon...

It was only natural I became a despairing recluse after she passed away.

I know she wants me to be happy but I can't oblige.

Even with the books doing well and living a more comfortable life; what does it matter when I'm without my Bette... I believe the time is near."

"Time for what John?"

"I had a dream last night; did I tell you?"

"No, you didn't"

"Bette was in it. She was running around this nursing home looking for something..."

"John, you okay? Kind of spaced out there."

"Oh, sorry. I forgot for a moment what she was looking for. I remember now. She was looking for a ticket."

"What kind of ticket?"

"I don't know. Boy you sure are nosy."

"Sorry, John."

After a bit John sat there and mouthed the words 'forgive me' with hand held to his chest.

Sarah nodded yes with a smile.

"I'm going to take a nap sweetheart. Will I see you later?"

"It is soon closing time for me but I will see you tomorrow with those leftovers...

" I can't wait. Now don't tell me. I want it to be a surprise."

"Copy that, chief."

"You sound like one of my characters."

"Talk about 'can't wait'. I'm going to the book store after work. Don't forget to autograph the book for me tomorrow?"

"I won't and it will be my pleasure."

'Thank you, John my old writer friend."

"I like that. Oh Sarah, one more thing.

When I'm gone to be with Bette I want you to know that all the royalties are going to Bette's favorite charity which benefits children."

"That's wonderful John. I'm sure Bette is pleased and proud.

By the way tell her to hold off on the summoning. We have more to talk about. Good night John."

"Good night Sarah. God bless."

*

Dear Sarah

A brief note before falling asleep to tell you I remembered the rest of the dream and wanted to write it down so I don't forget.

So Bette was running around here, there and everywhere looking for that ticket and she found it. It was punched. She started to cry and laugh, cry and laugh, cry and laugh.

'What's the matter, hon?' I asked.

'Oh I'm sad for Sarah.' She replied.

'What do you mean? Is she okay?'

'She's fine dear.'

'And her family?'

'Fine.'

'Then what is it love?'

'She will miss you, very much.'

'Why? I'm real tired and too old to be going anywhere.'

'No sweetheart not too tired or old for where you're going.

And that is why I'm happy.'

Well that's it Sarah. Maybe I will go to that place tonight in a dream with Bette. I'll tell you all about it tomorrow.

Sincerely

Love from the old writer.

*

John died in his sleep.

Sarah left work that day with the bought copy of John's book.

She kept the leftovers in the nursing home fridge. John would like other patients enjoying the food.

She is happy to know her friendship will continue with the old writer whenever she picks up his book.

Made in the USA
Middletown, DE
20 November 2017